His Christmas Pixie

By Darlene Tallman

Table of Contents

Copyright
Dedication
Acknowledgements
Prologue
Chapter One
Chapter Two
Chapter Three
Chapter Four
Chapter Five
Chapter Six
Chapter Seven
Chapter Eight
Chapter Nine
Chapter Ten
Chapter Eleven
Chapter Twelve
Chapter Thirteen
Chapter Fourteen
Chapter Fifteen
Chapter Sixteen
Epilogue
About the Author

Copyright

This is a work of fiction. Names, characters, places, and incidents are either the product of the author's imagination or used fictitiously, and any resemblance to actual persons, living or dead, business establishments, events or locales is entirely coincidental.
All rights reserved.
His Christmas Pixie
Copyright 2016 © Darlene Tallman
Published by: Darlene Tallman
Editor: Emily Kirkpatrick
Cover by Dark Water Covers
ALL RIGHTS RESERVED. This book contains material protected under International and Federal Copyright Laws and Treaties. Any unauthorized reprint or use of this material is prohibited. No part of this book may be reproduced or transmitted in any form or by any means, electronic or mechanical, including photocopying, recording, or by any information storage and retrieval system without express written permission from. Darlene Tallman, the author / publisher.

Dedication

This story is for my ride-or-die girls, who hopefully know how important they are to this journey we call life! For my Renée's-yes, I have two important women in my life named Renee. For my Debbie's-again, multiple women in my life named Debbie have "been there" with and for me over the years. And for Sandra, who didn't shy away from a sixteen-year-old "Yankee" that very first day we met. I love all of you more than words can say and am so very grateful that you were put on my path!

Acknowledgments

When I first read of this anthology, my mind started spinning and the beginnings of a story came to mind. I like women who have overcome the odds no matter what they are-be it an unplanned pregnancy, domestic abuse, a crappy family of origin. Being able to bring that to life in a way that people enjoy reading about is one of my goals as an author and I hope I have succeeded in this story.

I initially didn't think I'd have this one finished in time, but with a lot of encouragement from Cree, I pushed through, so I want to thank a woman whose encouragement has meant a lot since I pushed "publish" the very first time. I cannot wait until 2017 when I get to meet you in Dallas!

Emily "Eagle Eye" Kirkpatrick, who misses little and whose changes are (hopefully) making each one I write easier to edit as I take those previous tweaks and apply them to the next story. You took a chance on a newbie; glad you're along for the ride!

And for Tracie with Dark Water Covers who created the gorgeous cover-I foresee a lot of collaborating in the future with your talent!

Last but certainly not least, my betas-Pam, Joanne, Melanie, Kat, and Sherry-who have been with me since the first book and continue to offer great suggestions to make my perfectly imperfect characters more believable, while Mel takes my words and crafts some of the prettiest teasers I've ever seen that capture those words in a way that folks want to read what I've written!

Prologue

Six years, nine months ago

"Shit, Chessie, the condom broke! Now what?"

Six years, seven months ago

"How do I even know it's mine?"
"Um, well, the condom broke, remember asshole?"

"That means nothing, if you gave it up to me, you could have given it up to someone else."

With tears in her eyes, Chessie realized that the boy she was half in love with and had given her virginity to was in fact, an immature jackass. Great. Now what was she going to do? Her parents were going to kill her.

***

"Out! No daughter of mine will disrespect this family by getting pregnant!"

"Dad, where will I go?" she sobbed.

"Don't know, don't care. Call one of your friends

or something."

Six years ago

"Push! C'mon Chessie, you can do this! Push one more time-you've got this," her two besties said.

Looking at them both, she couldn't believe she had been blessed enough to have not one but two friends who cared enough to take her in when her parents kicked her out. The three of them were now roommates, and with Pam already having a little one, kids and sleepless nights were already on the schedule. She still wondered what Jason was up to, but knew that after he found out she had gotten pregnant from their one and only night together, he had bailed. She couldn't blame him, she was just eighteen and he had turned twenty-one a few months before that fateful night. She vowed that the only one she would love would be this little one trying to rip her in half.

Chapter One

Chessie couldn't believe it was only two weeks until Christmas. Two weeks until Jade turned six. Two weeks until she and the girls took a much-needed vacation. As she thought back over the past six years, she was, once again, grateful for the two friends and their parents who had taken her in when her mom and step-dad kicked her out. She was able to finish high school, and was now enrolled in night classes at the local tech school and working during the day at the diner, along with Pam and Fran. The three of them were hell on wheels, but the regulars loved them and the diner was always full to overflowing with customers.

Walking into the diner, she went to the back and grabbed her apron, pad and a few pens before she checked to see what section was hers today. As she passed by Pam, she saw her wiggle her eyebrows over toward section one, where she apparently had a new customer waiting. Hmm, wonder what that was about? Pam knew that after the hell she went through with Jason, no man was going to be on her radar ever again. It had taken the Thompsons and their lawyer to get Jade any kind of child support, which thankfully was an automatic thing since Jason was now in the military. She was lucky, too, that the insurance covered Jade because lordy, she had been a sickly baby! Shaking her head, she pasted a smile on her face and headed to the table Pam had indicated.

"Hi, I'm Chessie, and I'll be your waitress today. Can I start you out with some coffee, juice or soda?" she asked.

Warm, brown eyes looked up at her. "Um, coffee, black, please."

Momentarily taken back, she smiled and said, "Coming right up" before she beat feet to the back where the coffee pots were. Holy hell! Who on *earth* was that man? She hadn't had even an inkling of interest in anyone in over six years. One look at that guy and she was wanting to plant flowers around a white picket fence. *Shit shit shit*. Taking another deep breath, she returned with his coffee and a carafe, because he looked like someone who likely drank more than one cup and her section was filling up. Fast.

"Did you decide what you wanted?" she asked.

"I'll have the breakfast special, eggs sunny side up, white toast with butter and some grape jelly, no grits, hash browns with onions, and crisp bacon."

Well, he was a big guy so it stood to reason he could eat all of that, she thought, as she jotted it all down.

"And I'll take a water too, please," he said as she was walking away. Waving her hand to let him know she heard, she went and grabbed that, along with more napkins and placed them on his table before heading to the next one in her section. Man, it was hopping today-likely folks wanting to finish up their Christmas shopping.

"Hey Chessie! We want the usual, okay girl?"

"Yeah, sure, Mike. Coffee all around?"

"Yes, ma'am. You know us so well."

Putting in their order, she took a few minutes to think about the new guy sitting in her section. Who was he? Was he just passing through or did he live here now?

Chapter Two

Mack Corrigan looked at the waitress as she walked away. She was a cute little thing, with a pixie face and blonde hair streaked with pink. His interest piqued, he started listening to the other customers as they interacted with her. She seemed to give as good as she got, joking around and teasing the regulars she was serving. He wondered if she had a man in her life, then wondered why on earth a few words from a virtual stranger would have him thinking along those lines. Hell, he hadn't been interested in a woman for more than getting his dick wet in years, yet there was something about her that drew him to her. He didn't believe in insta-love, but lust? Hell yeah. Deciding that he wanted to get to know her better, especially since he was new in town, he waited until she came back with his food before he said, "Chessie? That's an unusual name for a beautiful woman like you."

Smiling, she said "It's short for Francesca, but only my mom called me that."

"Ah, I see. Well, my name's Mack and I'm new in town. Maybe you could show me some of the local sights later?"

"Um, well, I would like that but I've got class tonight."

Thinking quickly, he pulled out his phone and said "What's your number? I'll text you so you have mine and then maybe we can figure out a better time?"

She rattled off her phone number, intrigued at how this complete stranger was making her feel. She had honestly felt nothing for any of the men she had met since Jason. Even that jackass, whenever she had the misfortune to see him when he was home on leave, did nothing for her any longer. She figured that the trauma of getting pregnant the first time, then being kicked out and forced to grow up quick had stifled any kind of desire for a man in her life. Well, this could end quickly too once he found out she had a kid. "Uh, Mack, you'll find out soon enough anyhow, but I have a daughter and she's going to turn six on Christmas Eve. Just figured you might want to know because a lot of guys are not interested after they find that out and she's the most important thing in my life."

Sitting back, he took a good look at her–she was standing almost defensively as if she expected him to say something derogatory. "Look, I know you don't know me, but here's the thing, if you're a package deal you're a package deal. I'm okay with that, are you?"

Momentarily stunned because this was *not* how anyone else reacted, she could only stare at him. Those beautiful chocolate brown eyes showed interest, compassion and kindness. *Holy hell.* "Um, yeah, I'm okay with that, I just wanted you to know. I'll…I'll let you know what my schedule is, okay? I know the tree lighting is tomorrow night and I had planned to go there, would you like to go? We have a festival of sorts with booths and food and crafts; typical small-town stuff."

Smiling, he reached out and grabbed hold of her hand. "Yeah, I'd like that, what time should I meet you?"

"How about four? Jade is already out of school and tonight is the last night of classes until January for me, so I had planned to do some Christmas shopping in the morning."

"Four it is then. And Chessie? I look forward to it."

"Me too."

Heading to the kitchen area, she bumped Pam and motioned for her to follow her. In a few quick words, she told her what had happened and then had to slap her hand over her friend's mouth when she went to squeal. "Shut up! Oh my gosh, girl! You'd think no guy had hit on me before!"

"Well, they *have* but someone has always turned them down! What's different about this guy?"

"I don't really know. He's good looking in a rugged sort of way, but it's the look in his eyes. Very kind, understanding eyes and he didn't even flinch when I brought up Jade. You know she's a deal-breaker for most of the chuckleheads around here."

"Sweetie, that's their loss then. You're a helluva good mama to that little girl, and any man worth his salt wouldn't care that you are a single mom!"

"The only reason I'm halfway good at it is because of you and Fran and your parents. God knows that my step-dad was a jackass and of course, he had my mom under his thumb so deep that she couldn't or wouldn't stand up to him for me."

"Yeah, yeah, I love you too. Who would have thought that the two of us would get preggers and dumped? I am grateful to my folks, too, though, because hell, they had not only me, but you, throwing up all the time and crying. And then two little ones? Yep, we're blessed, that's for sure!"

Hearing the bell ding, they both headed back out into the diner, taking care of the customers who were finishing up and finding places for the new ones to sit. The three of them worked well together and she couldn't wait to get Fran's input on this guy.

Chapter Three

Done with classes for the day, Chessie hurried home so she could see Jade for a little while before her bath and bed.

"How's my sweet girl tonight? Did you have a good day with Grandma Sadie?" she asked her daughter once she found her in the playroom. "Mama!" Jade shrieked as she ran into her arms. "We went *Christmas* shopping for you and Aunt Pam and Aunt Fran but it's a 'prise."

Laughing at the little girl's enthusiasm, she said, "Well, we don't want to spoil it now, do we? I'm so glad you had fun today with Grandma Sadie and Sophie. Guess what we're doing tomorrow afternoon?"

"What?"

"Well, mama met a nice man today at work and he's going to meet us at the festival and watch the Christmas tree lighting. And maybe, we can talk him into going over to the snow mountain play area because I know a little girl who wanted to go sledding."

"A man, mama? Is it…is it my daddy?"

Sighing inside, because Jason had had nothing to do with the precious little girl, she said, "No sweetie, it's not your daddy. I'm sorry he doesn't come around, but I hope you know that it is not your fault at all! You've got so many people who love you–Aunt Pam, Aunt Fran, Grandma Sadie and Grandpa Sam, even your daddy's parents–all love you and know you are a very special little girl!"

"Daddy just doesn't know how to love, mama, that's what is wrong with him. What is the man's name we are meeting?"

"His name is Mack, but you'll call him Mr. Mack to be respectful, okay?"

"Yes, ma'am. Mama, can we read a story from my princess book after my bath?"

Looking at her daughter's sweet face, she said, "Absolutely. Do you want bubbles tonight?"

More shrieks hit her ears as Jade began doing the little dance she had learned at daycare. Most days, between the three women and the Thompsons, they didn't have to use daycare for either of the girls, but right now, with school out and the diner busier due to the holiday traffic,

Jade and Sophie had been there several days these past few weeks. Looking at the clock, she said, "Let's get this stuff cleaned up so we can get in the tub, okay?"

Later that night, relaxing with a glass of wine and her kindle, she thought about the day. It was quiet tonight-Pam had gone out on a date with a guy she met at the diner-hmm, could they be getting serious? It had been almost two months already and he was the only one in the picture. She sure hoped so-Pam deserved a decent man, and Fran was pulling a double on the overnight shift. Sophie was still at her grandparent's house, and Jade would go there in the morning so the girls could bake some Christmas cookies. Her thoughts wandered to the man she had met. Tall, rugged, handsome with dirty blond hair and those gorgeous brown eyes. A strong looking jaw with a hint of scruff. Not only had he piqued her interest, something that no one had done in years, he had left her a generous tip. She couldn't wait to see him again the next day. Hearing the ping of her phone, she opened it to find a text message.

Mack: Hey, it's Mack. I wanted you to have my number. And, I also wanted to tell you how glad

I was that I sat in your section today. I'm looking forward to tomorrow.

Holy shit! It was him! Realizing he couldn't see her and thanking God at the same time that he *couldn't* see her, she answered.

Chessie: Hey. Thank you for your tip today! That was very generous and completely unexpected. I'm glad I met you today, too, and am looking forward to tomorrow as well! I forgot to tell you, but they have a section called snow mountain and I have a little girl who wants to do some sledding, so dress warm!

Wondering if she should tell him about Jade, she decided to throw caution to the wind. In for a penny, in for a pound, right?

Chessie: About my daughter. She has Downs Syndrome. It's one of the reasons I don't really date. Most guys don't want to be bothered. I wanted you to know because, well, I felt something when we met and if I'm being honest, I don't want to get my hopes up for anything if it's a problem.

Mack: Pixie, I know we don't know each other well yet, but that's not an issue.

Chessie: Pixie? WTH?

Mack: You remind me of a pixie.

Chessie: Oh, okay. So, what brought you to Jenkinsburg?

Mack: Honestly? I missed small town living. My folks are gone and my brothers are scattered across the country. I remembered visiting my aunt years ago when I was a kid and decided to make a change.

Chessie: You have family in the area?

Mack: An aunt lived there and when she died, we inherited her property. My brothers had no interest so when the renters moved out, I decided to take over the property since she willed us her hardware store as well. I've got some plans for renovations on it so won't be too hands-on initially especially since she had a good team in place, but will be there frequently.

Ah, so he planned to stay! Interesting.

Chessie: Well, you'll find small town living is like living in a fishbowl sometimes. Everybody knows your business. Can be annoying, but most of the time, it's kind of nice, to be honest. I grew up here. My mom and step-dad still live here, but I live with my two best friends.

Mack: Can I ask how old you are, Pixie-girl?

Chessie: I just turned 24. How old are you?

Hearing her phone ring, she looked and he was calling! Holy shit. Well, they needed to get to know one another, she supposed.

"Hello?"

"Hey, Pixie. Figured it would be easier to call and talk. My fingers don't work on that small text keyboard so good."

Laughing, because she remembered he had large hands, she said, "I hear you. So, you didn't answer my question. How old are you?"
"I'm thirty-two. Is that a deal-breaker for you?"

"Um, no. Just to toss it out there, though, I haven't dated in a long time." *Like, since high school*, she thought.

"Why not? A beautiful woman like you?"

"Well, remember what I said about small towns? Being a pregnant, unwed teenager meant that most of the guys who asked me out only wanted one thing from me, and that wasn't happening. Plus, Jade was sick a lot when she was little, and between finishing high school, getting into college, working and her, there really wasn't time."

He thought for a minute and realized that this petite woman had faced some hard times, but she didn't sound bitter. He also recognized that he would have to move slow, but hoped that he wouldn't have to move too slow.

"Sounds like it was challenging for you, Pixie-girl."

"Ah, yeah. If it hadn't been for my two best friends and their parents, I know I wouldn't be where I am now."

"What about your parents? You said they live here?"

"My mom and step-dad? Yeah. Gosh, you ask all the tough stuff. When they found out I was pregnant, my step-dad kicked me out. Pam and Fran's parents took me in and I lived with them and finished high school and had Jade. They had their hands full! Pam was also pregnant at the same time, so they had two hormonal, crying, puking teens on their hands! They've been my family for the past six years. I don't even see my mom, although she knows about Jade. Honestly, I'm surprised Fran wanted to live with us because we were two hot messes."

"I saw how the three of you were today at the diner."

"Ha! Yeah, we were fortunate that their parents own the diner and they put us girls to work early on. The three of us generally work different shifts, but there are times when the three of us work at the same time and it's rather funny, if I say so myself!"

Mack wondered how he could tell her that he had heard of her from his former friend. He had served a tour with Jason, and while what he said about her was less than complimentary, the pictures he had seen that Jason's parents sent of the little girl had intrigued him. It was a win-win for him—he had his aunt's house to move into and he could meet the girl who had captivated him through pictures.

"Pixie-girl, I want to be honest with you. I served with Jason on a tour overseas and saw pictures of you and your little girl. Your smile and eyes captivated me and I knew, when the house became available, that I wanted to move here and get to know you."

Not knowing what to say, Chessie processed what he had just told her. Shit, if Jason had talked about her, it was probably in less than complimentary terms. They had dated while she was in high school and it wasn't until she turned eighteen that she had punched her v-card with him and look how that had turned out!

"Pixie-girl? You still there?" he asked cautiously.

"Uh…um, yeah. I'm not sure what to say, quite honestly."

"I wanted you to know. I know he comes home from time to time on leave to see his folks and didn't want you finding out that way. I really do want to get to know you and that little girl better."

"I'd like that, Mack. I'd like that a lot."

Turning the conversation to lighter subjects, they continued to talk for hours until she heard a soft cry from Jade's bedroom.

"Mack, I need to go. Jade sometimes has nightmares and I think she's having one now. I'll see you tomorrow?"

"Absolutely, Pixie-girl. You sleep well, okay?"

"You too. See you tomorrow."

Going into her daughter's bedroom, she saw her tossing and turning and crying. "Shhh, Mama's here, honey girl. I've got you. Shhh."

About an hour later, after she calmed her down, she finally made her way to her room where she got ready for bed. Fran wouldn't be home until morning, and Pam hadn't gotten home from her date yet. She fell asleep thinking about the handsome man she had met that day with beautiful chocolate eyes.

Chapter Four

Rushing home the next afternoon, she got changed into jeans, a warm sweater, and her boots, then got Jade ready to be out in the cold. This time of year was hard on the little girl-if they weren't careful, she would pick up everything that was going around. Thankfully, she had found a doctor who was okay using alternative treatment methods and they were slowly building up her immune system. "Are you excited, pumpkin?" she asked her daughter.

"Yes, Mama. Mama? Can we take Sophie with us? Grandma Sadie and Grandpa Sam won't go until later and Aunt Pam is working."

"Let me call, okay? I don't have a problem with taking her early with us and it will give you someone to play with, right?"

Making a quick call, she looked at her daughter and said, "Okay, let's roll! We need to get Sophie and head on over so we can meet up with Mr. Mack."

Hearing the excited squeals, she smiled. Jade was such a happy little girl.

Once at the festival, she texted Mack to see where they could meet and was pleasantly surprised when she saw him walking toward her. "Hey Pixie-girl. Who is this little sprite you have with you?" he asked, crouching down so he could look at the little girl eye-to-eye.

Giggling, Jade said, "I'm not a sprite, I'm Jade!"

"Well, hello, Jade, I'm Mack," he said, as he held out his hand to the little girl who was the spitting image of her mother with her blonde hair and blue eyes.

"Hi Mr. Mack. Mama told me we were meeting you today. This is my friend Sophie," she said, introducing him to the other little girl standing next to Chessie.

"Hi, Sophie. Are you girls ready to have fun?"

"Yes, sir."

Standing back up, he reached for Chessie's hand, drawing her close before he kissed her on the forehead. "Hey, Pixie-girl. You ready to have some fun?"

Looking up at him, she wanted to tell him that the fun she was thinking of didn't involve two little girls, but him in a bed. Blushing at her thoughts, she said, "Yeah. I am."

With Jade and Sophie holding hands and skipping a bit in front of them, he held her hand and then said, "Um, where are your gloves?"

"Oh! Well, with getting the girls put together, I guess I forgot them. Again. Bad habit of mine."

Laughing, he tucked her hand into his and then into his pocket to keep them warm. As they went by different booths on their way to snow mountain, he kept an eye out and when he saw what he was looking for, stopped and, despite her protests, got her a pair of fuzzy gloves and a matching pair of earmuffs. "There, now you really look like a snow pixie!" he said, dropping a kiss on the tip of her nose.

Good grief and gravy! This man was making her insides turn to goo. What had happened to her resolve? No men again. Ever. It had obviously gone by the wayside.

"Thank you, Mack. Does this mean you don't want to hold my hand anymore?"

Oh for the love of all things gold! Why on earth did she just say that??? Groaning inside, she chanced a look at him and saw him smirking at her, almost as if he could read her mind. "Nope. Just means that I want to make sure the hand I'm not holding stays warm!"

Finally reaching snow mountain, they got the two little girls sleds then trudged up the hill so they could watch them slide down, laughing and squealing. The next time they came up, giggling and covered in snow, she got her phone ready and shot a video of them as they went back down the hill, then sent it in a text to Pam and Fran, who would both get a kick out of how much fun they were having. On the third trip up, she saw that Mack had gotten an adult sled and, giving her a look, said, "I think we need to go down a few times ourselves, Pixie!"

Laughing, because she hadn't been on a sled in a few years, she made sure the girls were set and then climbed onto the sled in front of him. Oh. my. gosh! His arms wrapped around her making her feel a sense of security she hadn't felt in her life. "Okay girls, we'll give you a head start. Ready, set, go!" Mack said, watching the two little girls start down the hill. Leaning into her, he whispered, "You ready, Pixie-girl?"

Um, yeah. She thought it was probable that her ovaries had exploded watching him interact not only with her daughter, but also with the little girl she considered her niece. "Yeah, let's go and see if we can catch them!"

As they reached the bottom of the hill, just behind the girls, she could hear Jade giggling as she said, "Mama, we beat you and Mr. Mack! Does that mean we can have some hot chocolate now?"

"Sure, pumpkin. Let's get some hot chocolate and warm up for a few minutes. What else did you two want to do?"

"Can we build a snowman? And see Santa? And go pet the animals?"

Laughing because her daughter had specific ideas about what she wanted to do, she said, "Absolutely. We can do whatever you two want today, okay? Now, don't forget, when Grandpa Sam and Grandma Sadie get here, you girls will go with them."

Mack led the trio of girls to the covered tent where food and drinks were being sold. Taking "orders", he told Chessie to stay with the girls while he went and got their stuff.

"Mama, I'm having fun and I like Mr. Mack, he's really nice."

"Yes, he is sweetpea, yes he is."

They spent the rest of the afternoon on snow mountain and, if she had to say so herself, their snow people were the best out there. Mack had gone back to one of the stalls and bought some hats and scarves so they were all gussied up. Heading back to the food tent for yet another cup of hot chocolate, she saw the Thompsons headed their way, along with Pam and Fran.

"Hey y'all! Glad you caught up with us. These two have been keeping us busy. Mr. and Mrs. Thompson, Pam, Fran, this is Mack Corrigan. He just moved to town. Mack, this is my family."

Reaching his hand out, Mack shook Mr. Thompson's hand firmly, saying, "Pleasure to meet you, sir. Really enjoyed the meal I had at the diner yesterday, which is where I met Chessie."

"Corrigan. Are you by any chance kin to Vera Corrigan?"

"She was my aunt, sir. I just moved into her house."

"She was a wonderful woman, sorry for your loss, but we're always glad to have new folks in town."

While Mack talked to the Thompsons about his aunt and the house, Pam and Fran drew Chessie away.

"Girl, he is F-I-N-E!" Fran exclaimed.

Pam chimed in, "If I wasn't hooked on Derek, I would have stolen your section yesterday. Just saying!"

Chessie grinned. "Oh you two! So, he apparently knows Jason, and saw pictures of Jade and me. Said he was glad he was able to move here so he could meet me!"

"Really? Oh my *God* that's fantastic!" they both said.

"It's about time someone caught your eye, young lady!"

"Yeah, yeah. You both know that the guys around here are only interested in one thing and none of them wanted anything to do with me because of Jade."

"Doesn't seem to bother Mack, though," Pam mused.

"Nope. He's been great with both the girls this afternoon!"

Seeing the Thompsons and Mack walking toward them, she turned to her friends and grinned before she whispered, "He's hot! Holy hell, the thoughts that have been running through my head since meeting him yesterday would make a whore blush!"

With that, both of her friends burst into laughter, Fran doubling up.

"What's got you three cackling like hens?" Mr. Thompson asked.

"Uh…nothing, dad. Nothing at all," Pam choked out between her giggles.

"Well, we've got our area staked out for the lighting so all of you are more than welcome to sit with us, but we'll go ahead and take the girls now so you young people can wander around some more," he said.

"Sounds great-they've probably had their fill of hot chocolate, but other than that, they've been playing pretty hard and were making some noise about being hungry," Chessie told him.

"We'll get them fed. Chessie, do you have Jade's bag in your car?"

"Yes, I'll bring it to the tent on our way over if that's okay?"

"Works for us. Alright you little munchkins, let's let your mamas go play," he said to the two little girls.

"Okay, Grandpa Sam," Jade said before running to her mom for hugs and kisses.

"Be a good girl for Grandma and Grandpa, okay pumpkin?"

"Yes Mama. Love you!"

"Love you too, my sweet girl, to the moon and back!"

As the Thompsons walked away from them, she looked at Pam and said, "Is Derek meeting you here?"

"Yeah, he texted me a few minutes ago and said he'd find us. Won't be hard since I told him to look for the fuzzy-eared blonde!"

"Whatevs. Mack got me these because I forgot my gloves. Again."

Once again, Pam and Fran broke out in hysterical laughter. "Mack, she probably has a thousand pairs of gloves and we've lost count of how many headbands, ear muffs and hats she has misplaced," Fran said.

"Hey now, I don't 'misplace' them, I just forget to grab them is all!" Chessie said, trying to act indignant but failing as she started laughing.

"Uh, Aaron is meeting us too," Fran said.

"Aaron? I thought you guys were…" Chessie and Pam both said at the same time.

Interrupting them, Fran said, "We *were* and now we aren't. Clear as mud, right? We just had a few things we had to work out is all."

While they wandered back through the booths, Fran and Pam peppered Mack with questions. He answered them, understanding that their concern was their friend. Derek found them in the pottery booth, resulting in another round of introductions. Pam had only been seeing him for a short time, but she felt a connection and he didn't care that she was a single mom, something most of the other jerks she had dated eventually cited as their reason for breaking up. Slow and steady, though. She was tired of being burned.

"Fran! Hey Fran!" a voice called out. Turning, they saw a man coming through the crowd. "I wasn't sure I would find you!"

"Hey Aaron! Let me introduce you to Chessie's date. Aaron McCoy, this is Mack Corrigan. Mack, this is my boyfriend, Aaron."

"Nice to meet you, man," Aaron said, shaking Mack's hand. "Hey Derek! Good to see you!"

Chessie smiled inside-this was a good first date, they weren't alone and she had her besties there to help her get a read on this man.

"So, what do you guys want to do? We still have about two hours before they light the tree."

Mack looked at Chessie. He had loved holding her when they were sledding. "What about snow mountain? We can sled for a while before we feed these beautiful women we have with us."

"Oh hell yeah," Derek exclaimed.

The decision made, the group headed back over to snow mountain where they got the adult sleds and headed up the hill. Chessie was secretly thrilled because she would have his arms around her again. As they got seated on the sled and his arms came around her, he leaned in and whispered, "Pixie-girl, I'm having a great time and I hope you are as well."

Leaning back, she looked up and said, "Yeah. This is the most fun I've had in a long time, Mack. Thank you."

He couldn't resist kissing her nose before he said, "Let's see if we can beat these guys down the hill, yeah?" as he pushed off.

Her laughter rang out, and the sound of her giggles went straight to his gut. He knew it was crazy but there was something about the woman in his arms that had him thinking of forever.

A dozen or so treks up and down the hill later, the group decided to find some food before they headed to the tent to watch the tree lighting. It was a town tradition to do it two weeks before Christmas, even though the rest of the town was decorated to the nth degree. Heading into the food tent, they were trying to figure out what they wanted to eat when they heard, "Well, well, well, what a cozy looking group!" and turning, they saw a very drunk Jason, his arm slung around a skanky looking brunette. "Corrigan! Guess you liked what you saw in those pictures, huh?" He sneered as he said, "I would say 'enjoy' but it's not that good, trust me."

Absolutely mortified, Chessie looked down, completely missing the looks of rage that came over the faces of the three men at the ugly things spewing out of Jason's mouth. Pam and Fran, seeing her distress, moved closer to her, while

Mack walked up to the inebriated man and said, "Really? You've got no call to say things like that about Chessie. None at all. In fact, this is a family event, so you showing up drunk off your ass shows the type of man you really are. Now, before you end up going back with a busted face, I suggest you leave. Now. Your presence is not wanted." Turning back, he saw the dejected look on Chessie's face, which did something to his heart. He walked over to her, letting Derek and Aaron deal with Jason, who was continuing his obnoxious spewing, and lifting her chin, he leaned in and quietly said, "Chessie? Look at me, sweetheart. I know he is a jackass and I don't buy what he's trying to sell, okay? I don't know what's happening with us, but today has been the best day of my life, and his words mean nothing."

Smiling slightly, she said, "I'm sorry, Mack. I wasn't thinking about the fact that he would be here."

"Not your place to apologize, sweetheart. You've done nothing wrong. Now, let's go get something to eat so we can find that little sprite," he said before he kissed her forehead. Man, he couldn't wait to claim her lips but now wasn't the time or the place. Soon.

Chapter Five

Conversation over dinner was stilted at first, with the guys still angry at Jason's intrusion and comments, and Chessie still embarrassed at how he denigrated her in front of Mack. Soon, though, as they started talking about Christmas, everyone loosened up and decided to enjoy the festivities.

"So, Pixie-girl, what does that little sprite want Santa to bring her?" Mack asked.

Laughing, she said, "What *doesn't* she want him to bring? Actually, she only asked for two things–a live kitty cat and a baby doll."

"And is Santa going to deliver?"

She looked at Pam, then said, "Yeah, because apparently she and Sophie *both* want live kitties and baby dolls this year, we decided to adopt two kittens from a local rescue. They're holding them for us until next week. And Santa and his helpers, also known as Aunt Pam, Aunt Fran and me, will be redoing their playroom to put in a kitchen for them to 'cook' for us, and Mr. Thompson has built beds for their baby dolls. I have to finish crocheting the blankets for the dolls' beds, and Aunt Fran is working on something special as well. They really don't ask for much, and they're both so good we can't resist spoiling them a bit. With Jade's birthday being on Christmas Eve, we don't want her to feel short-changed, so we had her give us two lists."

"So this time of year is doubly special for her, then, huh?" he asked.

"Yes. She loves that she shares her birthday with Jesus, and even though we've tried to tell her differently, she sticks to that story."

"You mentioned college, what are you majoring in?"

"Well, I'm doing somewhat of a hybrid major. I need something that will allow me to work but be available for Jade if she's sick, so I am taking the courses needed to be an editor, and also doing a graphic arts program."

"Don't let her fool you. She's damn good at what she does! She is already designing book covers for several authors, and is already editing for them as well," Pam said.

"Really? I bet that gives you the flexibility you need."

"It really does. And, because the three of us live together, I still have adult interaction. Plus, working at the diner, I get out."

Looking at her watch, Fran said, "We need to head on over if we're going to be there in time to see the tree lit up. You know how the girls get!"

Laughing, because those two girls loved Christmas and all it entailed, Chessie said, "Yeah, we better get a move on!"

As they made their way through the crowd toward the tent that the Thompsons had set up, Mack grabbed Chessie's hand and pulled her close to him. "You okay, Pixie-girl?"

"Yeah. Actually I am, now. Thanks for sticking up for me earlier, Mack."

"My pleasure."

They heard the girls before they saw them, then had to stop as two little girls came barreling out to their mothers, giggling and laughing. Shouts of mommy and mama were heard by the group, as Sophie and Jade both tried to tell them everything they had done since leaving them. "Girls, girls, one at a time! It sounds like you've had some cookies, dinner, and got to see Santa?"

Jade looked at her mom and said, "Yes, Mama! Santa said he knew I was a special little girl and that since my birthday was the *same night* as he came, I would probably get what I asked him for this year! Can you believe it?"

Smiling down at the face that was so precious to her, she said, "Yeah, pumpkin, I can believe it. You were my best Christmas present ever!"

Mack smiled at the picture they made, with Chessie crouched down in front of her daughter and Jade's arms wrapped around her mother's neck. They were forehead to forehead and nose to nose and without thinking twice, he pulled out his phone and took a couple of pictures. He knew it was early days and that Chessie had no clue how he was feeling, but he had an idea for a special gift for them.

"Ah, there you all are! We wondered if you were going to make it in time," Sam said. "Boys, we've got plenty of places to sit, and if you want chairs, we can run over to the diner and grab some chairs."

"Dad, we'll do what we've always done, sit on the blankets on the ground. I know you brought the air mattress so we'll be fine, right y'all?" Fran asked.

With everyone agreeing, they quickly chose their spots, Mack pulling Chessie to sit in front of him. Once they were settled, Jade climbed onto her mother's lap. He could feel the contentment flowing through him and felt that he had finally come home.

Chapter Six

Damn, she liked being held by him! And, she knew she was affecting him if the warmth she felt pressing against her ass and low back was any indication. Holy hell. He was apparently big all over! Nope. Not going there.

"What're you thinking about, Pixie-girl?"

Oh hell. Hoping that the colder air hid her blush, she said, "Um, nothing much, really."

He chuckled; he had felt her tense up and knew that despite his best efforts, she could feel his erection pressing into her. "Well, I've never been told it's nothing much, sweetheart, so this is a first for me!"

Realizing he was teasing her, she leaned her head back and grinned. "I was thinking about how safe and secure I feel being held in your arms. And how that makes no sense because we just met. Other than that, I'm not saying!"

"Ah, she gets sassy, eh?"

"Perhaps. Feisty sometimes, too," she said, grinning.

Yeah, he'd like to have her all feisty. In his bed. Damn, now he was harder than he was before, if that was possible.

"You okay back there, Mack? You're squirming a bit."

Leaning in and nipping her earlobe, he whispered, "Just thinking about how I like your feistiness and can't wait to have it in my bed."

Fuck. Fuckity fuck fuck fuck. He couldn't really say that to her now, could he? And, wait a minute! Why was she entertaining those thoughts? She hadn't been physically interested in *anyone* since Jason. Not a blip. Not a jot. Nothing. Yet this man came into her life a day ago and she was thinking about it with him? Yep. Off the deep end.

"I...I'm not sure what to say to that, Mack! I mean, I've...that is...isn't this moving kind of fast?" There. She'd said it. Put it out there.

"Maybe on one level, yes. But not on another. Can I tell you a story? My parents met when he stopped to help her change her tire. They were married within six weeks of meeting and were married for almost thirty years when they died."

"Wow. Well, I think the Thompsons were the same way."

"So, it *can* happen that fast."

Right before she was going to respond, she saw their mayor head to the podium for his annual speech. She shared a look with Pam and Fran, wondering if this year he would change it up a bit.

"Hello, friends and neighbors and thank you for coming to this year's Christmas tree lighting," the major started.

Nope. He was going down the same road he always did, thanking the local businesses for their donations, the townspeople for their support in the last election, and putting in a plug for snow mountain, which would stay up until winter ended. After his ten-minute spiel, she nudged Jade and said, "C'mon, sweetie, we need to stand up! It's almost time."

Mack helped them both up, then had Jade giggling and Chessie's heart falling fast when he scooped the little girl up and onto his shoulders.

"Oh! Thank you Mr. Mack! Now I can see everything!"

Sophie, seeing her friend up on Mr. Mack's shoulder, looked at Derek, who scooped her up and put her on his shoulders. With the two women standing in front of their "men", and Fran cuddled into Aaron, they watched the tree lighting while the local high school band played a medley of Christmas carols.

"Beautiful. Absolutely beautiful," Chessie breathed out.

Leaning down, Mack whispered in her ear, "Yes. Yes, you are."

Chapter Seven

Once the lighting was done, the adults pitched in to get everything put up and take the tent down.

"Um, Mack, I need to go to my car and get Jade's bag. She's going to spend the night over at the Thompsons."

"Okay. I'll go with you because I don't want you walking by yourself."

As they walked to her car, she was thinking about their afternoon. It had been a great time, one of the best ones she had ever had. Reaching her car, she unlocked it then grabbed Jade's bag and favorite stuffed animal, a penguin. "We'll just meet over at the diner; they gave the girls a light snack but will feed them dinner now. Is that okay?"

"Spend more time with you? Yes, that's absolutely fine with me," he responded, taking the bag from her and slinging it over his shoulder while he grabbed her other hand.

Reaching the diner, they entered and immediately found everyone. The diner was open twenty-four hours a day, and it seemed that others had had the same idea. Thankfully, there was a family only section, which the Thompsons had added several years back, so they had no waiting. Seeing how busy the place was, Chessie wondered if perhaps she and the girls should offer to help. But she didn't want to ask, because if the answer was "yes" she was afraid she might cry.

"Girls, I know it's busy in here tonight, but all three of you are off. The only thing you're allowed to do is go get our drinks, okay?" Sam said, after he saw the looks the three women had exchanged. "We appreciate everything the three of you do to help us keep this place going, but y'all deserve some relaxation and tonight's the night! Now tomorrow morning is a totally different story," he laughed.

"Thanks, dad."

"Thanks Mr. Thompson."

"Chessie, love, you should know by now to call us Mom and Dad or Sam and Sadie. When you say, 'Mr. Thompson' I swear I look for my own father!"

Blushing slightly, she nodded and said, "Yes, sir. I mean, dad."

As the girls got the drink orders and went to the back to get those together, Mack took the opportunity to ask Derek and Aaron about Jason. "Is he always like that around her? How can he treat the mother of his child like that?"

Derek answered for the two of them. "She may or may not tell you, but he denied that Jade was his, and she had to go through hell to get anything from him for that sweet little girl. And yes, ever since she came up pregnant, he's been an absolute ass towards her. He has been banned from the diner completely, and if it weren't for the fact his folks are genuinely nice people, I think someone would have beaten him to death. She's a good girl and didn't deserve the hand she was dealt."

"Ah, but she's shown them all," Aaron piped in. "She graduated near the top of her class, and even knowing that Jade would be born with Downs, she chose to continue the pregnancy. Her step-dad, and by proxy her mom, disowned her completely. Yet here she is, almost done with college, working her ass off here, and raising that little girl."

Mack sat back and thought about what they had just shared. He had the distinct impression that there had been no one since Jason, which would explain her hesitancy and fear about how fast things seemed to be moving with the two of them. He would have to show her he was in it for the long haul, not just a piece of ass.

About that time, the girls came back with their drinks, along with some bread and dipping sauce. "We hope no one minds, but we figured it would be easier to order the pasta for everyone," Fran said. "If anyone wants something different, let me know and I'll run back into the kitchen and change the order."

With everyone agreeing that pasta was fine, Pam asked who wanted salad and then the three girls went off again to get the salads fixed up and brought out to the table.

Looking down the table, Mack said, "Sam? I thought the girls were 'off' tonight?"

Sam looked around and started laughing. "Y'know, they do this same thing every time we come in as a family to eat! And, it just dawned on me that they did it again. Sneaky women."

Over dinner, the group talked and laughed, with the two little girls chattering excitedly about what they hoped Santa would bring them. As they finished up, Fran looked around and asked about dessert, then before anyone could say yes or no, darted to the kitchen and brought out a death by chocolate cake.

"Mmm, my favorite," Chessie murmured.

"Yeah, girl, I know. We make several every day and if memory serves, you have a piece *every day*," Pam said.

"That's right, tell all my secrets! Just you wait, missy," Chessie joked. "Derek, anything you wanna know, just ask me or Fran, we'll fill you in, okay?"

"What? Wait a minute now, if we're spilling secrets…"

"You wouldn't dare! Okay, okay, I'll behave. For now."

Mack watched Chessie with great interest. Whatever Pam was going to share had her blushing. As the group finished up, the girls cleaned the table as best as possible despite

Sam's protests. "Look, Dad, the least we can do is try and lighten up their load. They're slammed out there and it's not fair for us, the owners and friends, to come in and leave them with a mess," Fran said. "Besides, we take pride in this place, it's ours too, and knowing we can help our employees out, even a little bit, means a lot to us."

"Yeah, Dad, leave your girls alone!" Chessie said, as she gathered up plates and silverware.

"Chessie, I think that's the first time you've called me that, sweetheart. Means more than you'll ever know."

"Well, you *have* been a dad to me these past six years. I don't remember my real dad and we all know that my step-dad wasn't one to me, unless a dad treats his child like an indentured servant, so it's time, don't you think?" Chessie said, dropping a kiss on the top of Sam's head as she walked by. She didn't expect him to stand up and draw her into a hug, and she definitely didn't expect to hear what he said next.

"Sweetheart, from the first time you came into my daughters' lives, I've loved you like you were my own. Sadie has as well. You are as much our daughter as Pam and Fran are, and that little girl is our granddaughter, just like Sophie."

Feeling the tears threaten, Chessie looked up at him and said, "Thank you. I love you both so very much and am grateful that I have you guys in my corner."

With the room cleaned up and ready for more diners, the group went out and paid. A minor squabble ensued as Sam tried to pay for all of their dinners, but the other three men won, with each of them tipping the waitresses working even though they didn't serve them. As they prepared to go their separate ways, Chessie walked over to Jade and leaning down, gathered her daughter in her arms. "I love you, pumpkin. Be a good girl for Grandma and Grandpa, okay?"

"Yes, Mama. I love you too."

Chapter Eight

Mack knew he wanted Chessie with an ache deep inside. The question was, did she feel the same way? As he walked her to her car, he said, "Pixie-girl, I know this is fast, but I want you. If you want to wait longer, that's okay, but tonight, I would like to hold you all night long."

Oh.emm.gee! How on earth had he read her mind. Shit. Damn. Fuck. She wanted him too, more than she had ever wanted Jason. And, she felt deep inside that it wasn't a one-off thing with Mack. Something about how he looked at her and how gentle he was when he held her hand or pulled her close.

"O-okay. Um, well, there's no other way to say it except straight out. I haven't been with anyone since Jason, over six years ago. Is…is that a problem?" she stammered.

"No, my Pixie-girl. I hate how he treats you and the guys said he's like that all the time, but I'm glad that I'll be the last one in your life."

Holy shit! The last one? As her inner cheerleader woke up and began cheering, loudly, she simply said, "The last one?"

"Yes, sweetheart, the last one who will ever kiss you, make love to you, fuck you."

With all systems firing at his words, she stopped and looked at him. "Are you for real? This…this kind of thing doesn't happen to girls like me, Mack."

"What do you mean 'girls like you'?"

"Girls who have kids."

"Chessie, look at me," he said, waiting until she looked up at him. "I know it's fast. I know that you cannot fathom how I am feeling right now. But I knew from the moment I saw you that you were the one for me. Maybe it had to do with seeing the pictures that Jason's parents sent. Maybe it had to do with how you are with your friends and the folks you serve at the diner. I don't know. And, I don't rightly care. I want you. Under me. Over me. In front of me. For now and for always. Eventually, you'll understand the depth of my feelings."

With that said, he drew her close and, cupping her face with one hand, lowered his mouth to hers. "Let me in, Pixie-girl, I have a need for a taste," he murmured.

Opening her mouth, Mack swooped in and soon, their tongues were tangled in a dance older than time. As he nipped, licked and sucked her lips and mouth, he felt her melt into him. Knowing his body was already reacting to her nearness, he pulled her closer so she could feel what she was doing to him and was satisfied when he heard the moans coming from the back of her throat. Finally coming up for air, he continued kissing her face, nose, forehead, before he leaned in and sucked on her earlobe and nuzzled her neck.

"I have to work the breakfast shift tomorrow; do you…do you want to come over to my place? I'm ninety-nine percent sure that Fran went to Aaron's house and I think Derek went home with Pam," she asked hesitantly.

Looking down at her, he kissed her nose and said, "I'd love to. I told you already, I want to hold you tonight. Nothing else."

Breathing a sigh of relief, she said, "Okay, then follow me and try to keep up!"
"Ah, feisty pixie shows up once again!" he laughed.

"Maybe. It must be the season or something."

"I'm thinking it's 'or something' Pixie-girl."

Headed to her house with Mack following in his truck, she thought about the last two days. *Two days?* Who in their ever-loving mind falls for someone in two days?

Why you do her inner cheerleader said, already fixing up the pompoms that had been sitting in storage for a long time. *He's the kind of guy who ticks all your boxes so don't blow it!* Yeah yeah. Reaching the house, she pulled into the garage, grateful that they had a three-car garage because sometimes, the weather was horrible during the winter.

As they went in, she saw Pam and Derek sitting in the family room getting ready to watch a movie. "You guys want company or do you want to be alone?" she asked.

"Company's fine. We'll be alone later and since Pam is off tomorrow, we'll be together then too," Derek responded.
"Wait, how did you get a day off?"

"Hahahahaha, I threatened to quit."

"Again? Dang girl, one of these days, Dad is going to call your bluff and then what?"

"He knows me. You've got the morning shift and Fran took the afternoon. He actually said he's going to do that with us through Christmas. We'll only have a few days where we're all together. That way, we can all get some time off, and the teenagers working over the break can make some money."

"I love that man! He always thinks of everyone!" Chessie said.

"Mack, would you like something to drink? I want to change really quick if that's okay, but will grab them on my way back out."

"Water's fine, Pixie-girl, and I'll go grab it. Do you two need anything else?" he asked, looking over at Pam and Derek.

"Naw, man, we're good," Derek said.

Chessie hurried up and changed into a pair of sweatpants and a t-shirt, and changed into fuzzy socks. Her feet still felt frozen from tramping around outside for hours. Shit, if Mack was going to stay, he didn't have anything to change into! Oh well, they'd cross that bridge when they came to it, she thought, heading back to the family room.

"Okay, so what are we going to watch?" she asked as she headed to the couch Mack was sitting on, giving a small gasp when he reached up and pulled her close to him.

"There's an original Christmas movie on the Hallmark Channel," Pam said.

As they all settled in to watch the movie, Chessie was very aware of the man she was curled into. He had his arm wrapped around her shoulders and was idly playing with the tips of her hair. Surrounded by his warmth, she started dozing off.

"Pixie-girl? C'mon sweetheart, you fell asleep," she heard from far away.

"Mmmm."
"C'mon beautiful, let's get you to bed," Mack said, laughing. Pam and Derek had already headed off to her room, and he had enjoyed the feel of the petite woman snuggled up against

him and hadn't wanted to move. Helping her up, he kept hold of her hand as he headed in the direction she had gone earlier, hoping her room was here somewhere.

"Mack, it's the last door, straight ahead," she finally said once she realized he didn't know where to go. Entering the room, he closed the door behind them, then looked at her. "Uh, well, I need to change for bed. The bathroom's through that door over there. I don't have…I mean…well, hell…I know you're not going to sleep in your jeans but…"

Realization dawned on him when he heard her stammering. "Pixie-girl, I'll sleep in my boxers and T-shirt, yeah?"

"O-okay. That's good. Um, I'll be right back out, okay?" she said, going into the bathroom and shutting the door. Making quick work of her evening routine, she put on a sleep set, grateful it was a cute one at least, before she came back out of the bathroom to see him standing there. "Uh, I put a new toothbrush on the sink counter for you."

Smiling, he reached down and brushed a curl behind her ear before kissing her forehead. "I'll be back out in a few minutes."

She climbed into bed and turned on the television. This would be a first–sleeping with someone other than Jade. And, there would be no sex! *But I sure hope there's some more kissing because he can definitely kiss!*
As Mack came out of the bathroom, she looked at him and said, "I hope the left side is okay? I'm used to sleeping on the right side."

Hell, I'm just happy to be in the same bed as she is so any side is okay! Mack thought. "The left side is fine, Pixie-girl. Did you want me to go grab some water?"

Water would put out one of the fires that were raging! "Uh, yeah, that would be great!"

Damn, he was built. Broad, muscular shoulders with a few tats peeking out from under his T-shirt sleeves. Trim waist, nice muscular legs, and that ass! Holy shit, when he turned to go get the water, she saw a nice, tight ass. Mmhm. He was definitely one hundred percent man.

Crawling in on the left side, he reached out his arm and pulled her close so they were laying face-to-face. "Hey Pixie-girl," he whispered, kissing her forehead. "Thank you for this. I know this is all fast, but I promise you, nothing is going to happen. At least, not tonight."

And…now her inner cheerleader was getting out the bullhorn!

Smiling at him, she reached her hand up and cupped his jaw while her thumb stroked his cheek. "Mack, if I didn't want you here, I would have said no."

"So, are you still sleepy?" he asked.

"Mmm, no not really it seems my little nap has revived me a bit," she said.

Weaving his hands through her hair, he pulled her close before whispering, "Then let's make out for a while, yeah?"

"Okay" she said before slanting her head and placing her lips against his.
Soft. So fucking soft. And full.

Content to just lick and nibble on his lips, she didn't resist when his tongue touched hers. Tongues tangling, gently and then with more passion, she pressed closer to him, aware that all that separated them were his T-shirt and boxers and her pajamas.

"Mmm…I've been waiting to do this, my pixie," he whispered.

Hell, how could he still talk she wondered.

He pressed her back so he was partially over her, tangling their legs, as his hand caressed her shoulders and side, skimming the side of her breast.

She could feel his arousal pressing against her thigh, and thought her inner cheerleader was going to go insane, doing jumps and cartwheels. "Mmm…feels good Mack."

"Yes, you do. Can't wait until we take this further, but I'm a patient man," he said before claiming her lips again.

Seconds, minutes, hours–she didn't know how long they spent kissing. He found her spots on her neck that made her squirm and she found that his slight scruff was as much of a turn-on as his lips and hands.

"Pixie-girl, we need to stop before I can't," he finally said.

Sigh. "Yeah, I agree. Can I tell you something?" she asked.

"You can tell me anything. I'm a huge fan of honesty."

"I don't think I've ever been this turned on in my life," she said, blushing slightly.

"And…I am in the same boat, my sweet pixie, trust me!" he responded, giving her a final kiss that took her breath away before he settled her against his chest. "Now sleep. You have to work tomorrow."

Chapter Nine

Waking up the next morning, Chessie realized that next to having Jade, yesterday and last night had been the best day she had ever had and it was due to the man who was now spooning her. He had treated her with care and respect and that ticked a few more boxes for her. She went to get up and felt his arms tighten around her waist.

"Morning, Pixie-girl," he said, voice raspy with sleep.

"Good morning," she said. "Gotta get up and shower and get ready for work."

"I hate to let you go. I think this is the best I've ever slept."

"Me too. Then again, I've never slept with anyone other than Jade."

He thought about what she had just said. She gave him a first as well and he decided she needed to know.

"Chessie, I know we both have a past, but this is the first time I've slept with a woman. So, we were each other's first in something and that is pretty special, don't you think?"

"Yeah it is. Thank you, Mack. I've never been treated so well by someone."

Giving her a quick kiss and a light smack on the ass, he said, "Now, go get ready before I forget I'm trying to be patient and keep you in bed all day, showing you how I feel!"

Giggling, she got out of bed and grabbed clean clothes before heading into the bathroom to shower and get ready.

"I need coffee, Pixie-girl, so I'll meet you in the kitchen," he said.

"We have it on a timer so it should be ready. I won't take too long."

Heading out to the kitchen, Mack saw Derek. "Hey man. Maybe we can make breakfast for the girls?"

"Yeah, was about to see what they had. I know Chessie works this morning. Pam's in the shower right now. We're going to do some shopping," Derek responded.

"Yeah, Chessie is getting ready as well," Mack told him, head already in the refrigerator.

"Well, we have eggs, bacon and bread. How about scrambled eggs, bacon and toast?"

"Yeah, that should work," said Derek as he got out the pans and set the oven up for the bacon.

As they worked together making breakfast, they talked about the girls, what they did for work, Christmas, how Mack liked small town living. When Chessie and Pam got into the kitchen, they found the table set and the food ready to serve.

"Hey now, I could get used to this!" Pam cried, going over to Derek and giving him a kiss.

Grinning, Chessie said, "Absolutely!" before kissing Mack. "Thanks, guys!"

Over breakfast, the couples talked about the upcoming holiday and how the little girls were going to be so excited. Mack watched how animated Chessie got talking about Jade and her "lists". They had decided that they would celebrate her birthday on Christmas Eve, then go to midnight mass, before "Santa" arrived. That way, she got her day.

"I think that's been the hardest part of her having a birthday on Christmas Eve," Chessie said. "She knows it will likely only be family, but I've invited her classmates, so maybe a few will show up. I think as she gets older, I may do a party on another day so her friends can come. She goes to so many parties and loves having fun and I want her to have the same."

"Girl, if you'll give me the phone numbers, I'll start sending out texts and see if I can get any RSVPs," Pam said.

"That works for me! Thanks! Okay, you guys cooked so we're going to clean up before I head out," she responded.

As Mack and Derek sat there talking, the girls made light work of cleaning up the kitchen. The guys had done a lot of it as they cooked, so there really wasn't much.

"Are you guys getting the tree today?"

"Yeah, we thought we'd get two, one for the house and a smaller fake one for the girls' playroom. And, we're going to work on the playroom today so it's a good thing we can lock the door. Derek had an idea to put the kitchen in one area, then a 'living room' with a small television and dvd player in another. Kind of like a mini-house. Do you think they'd like something like that?"

"Oh hell yes they would! Can you see their faces? Let's put shiny wrapping paper on the door with a big bow and a tag that says 'To Jade and Sophie from Santa and friends' too! Maybe a loveseat? Bookshelf? Lamp? They'd have their own little 'house' and I think they'll love it!"

Mack, hearing how enthusiastic Chessie was about the project, looked at Derek and said, "I can help if you need it."

This time, Pam answered, saying, "It's all hands on deck and we cheerfully accept any and all help! Dad is coming over today to paint while mom keeps the girls busy. We're going to do each wall a different color so they can differentiate. As they get older, we'll change the room accordingly."

"Then it's a plan. And…I have to go; you know the morning crowd has been off the charts lately!"

As Mack walked her out to her car, she looked up at him and said, "Thank you, Mack. You don't know how much all of this means to me."

Drawing her close, he leaned down and kissed her forehead. "I think I have an idea, my Pixie-girl."

After a kiss that was sweet but hot, Chessie headed to the diner.

Chapter Ten

Chessie stopped for a few minutes to grab a quick drink and stretch-the morning rush had been insane with people waiting for tables. Tips had been good and she and Fran were already planning what they were going to do once their shift was done. With Pam, Derek, Mack and their dad working on renovating the girls' playroom, she and Fran had been tasked with finding the furniture and things to make it into a "house" inside. They had googled kitchens and found one at a store in the next town, and planned to grab a quick lunch then go and get it, along with all the accessories. She couldn't wait to see Jade and Sophie's little faces on Christmas morning! They knew something was up because their toys had been put in their rooms and the playroom door was now locked, but they had absolutely no idea what "Santa" had planned. Taking a deep breath, she headed back out to the floor; just another hour to go.

"Hey, you'll never guess what just happened," Fran said, coming around the corner.

"What?" Chessie asked.

"When Mr. Johnson overheard what we were doing for the girls, he left us two hundred dollars to get stuff! He said he wanted to be part of the 'Santa' gift and since he doesn't have any family, this was the next best thing!"

"Oh my goodness! We'll be able to get a little area rug for the 'living room' area and maybe small tv trays! Plus, the kitchen accessories. This is going to be so much fun!" Chessie responded.

"Can't wait! Meanwhile, over at table three, they'd like more coffee," Fran dead-panned.

"Ha! Yeah, was just headed back out there."

Walking over to table three, she grabbed a new pot of coffee. "Hey, y'all, heard you needed topping off! Sorry for the slight wait, I've been talking all morning and was starting to sound a bit croaky!" she told the table as she began topping off their coffees. Seeing that their water glasses were half full, she said, "Need water too? I'll go grab it for you."

"Naw, darlin', just the coffee," the man said. "And maybe your phone number."

"Ah, I'm seeing someone," she said.

"No harm in trying, is there?" he shot back.

"Not at all. Just being honest with you. Was there anything else you needed?"

"Aw leave her be Marvin! No, young lady, just the check when you get it ready, okay?" said the older man.

"Give me a few and I'll bring it back. You can either pay up at the register or I can handle it for you, whichever is easiest for you."

With that, she went and processed their ticket and then brought it back to the table. The man the older one had identified as Marvin said, "Listen, I meant no offense…"

"None taken. Are y'all here to visit the winter festival area? There are a lot of neat booths for one-of-a-kind gifts."

"Just passing through. Good food, though, so whenever we are in the area, we'll stop back."

"Fantastic! We love repeat customers and actually have quite a few who stop by to and from their vacation destinations!" she said cheerfully. *Man, this guy was giving her the heebie-jeebies!*

"Here you go, miss," the older man said, handing her the money along with their ticket. "Keep the change."

"Thank you. Safe travels!" she said, taking a few of their empty plates and heading back to the table.

With the breakfast rush over, she and Fran set about restoring order to the dining room. The busboy had called in sick, which had left them a bit short-handed, especially with Pam being off, but somehow they had managed. No one was ill-tempered and everyone showed an extreme amount of patience. In fact, there were several times that regular customers offered up their empty seats to those waiting so folks didn't have to wait long.

As the next shift came in, she took off her apron, counted her tips and went back to give some to the cook. He had worked his ass off, getting orders out in record time and not making any mistakes. "Hey Joe, thanks for today, it was crazy!" she said, walking up to him. "Here's your take, it was a good day on the floor for us!"

"Ah, Chessie-girl, you know you don't have to do that! Sam and Sadie pay me well and you girls don't have to tip me too!" he said, pushing her hand away.

"Pssh, Joe, I know you've been saving to get Alice that ring. Put it towards that, okay? It's Christmas time! Don't steal my opportunity to be a blessing to someone!" she mock growled.

Seeing that the young woman wasn't going to back down, he took the proffered money, then looked at her wide-eyed. "Uh, Chessie-girl, you realize how much you gave me?"

"Yep. I told you we were blessed today out there. You had to know we were busier than normal?"

"I did, kind of, but you know how I cook by now. I have trays of bacon always going, and as soon as one pan of scrambled eggs is done, I usually have another one ready to go so all I really have to do is the toast and the specialty eggs."

Ha! She loved that he called over-easy and sunnyside up "specialty eggs". He had done that for all the years she had known him. Reaching up, she kissed his cheek and said, "Thanks again, Joe. You are so appreciated. Now, shop for that beautiful wife of yours!"

"Yes, ma'am! Can't wait to see her face and I do believe that what you gave me will get it out of the store!"

"Well, I can probably ensure that one," Fran said, walking into the kitchen. "Here's your portion of my take as well. You can't say no. It's Christmas."

As Joe looked at the two young women who he had watched grow up, he got a little choked up. They knew how he had struggled when Alice got sick, and had pitched in working the kitchen, giving him their checks so he could stay home. They were the granddaughters he had never had, all three of them, and they were always looking out for him and his wife. Pulling them both close, he kissed their heads and said, "Love you girls. Now get outta my kitchen before you break the golden rule!"

"What's that?"

"There's no crying in the kitchen!"

Laughing, both girls hugged him again and left the kitchen, grabbing their purses and coats to head out for their shopping extravaganza.

Chapter Eleven

Mack looked at the room in amazement. All the walls were painted and the kitchen that Chessie and Fran found went perfectly in the far corner. On the opposite corner, a small entertainment center held a television, game console and the movies the little girls already owned. A small area rug was in front of the entertainment center, and they had recovered a loveseat that a friend had for the girls to sit on. They had two small end tables, making the area look like a living room. Behind that, they had built bookshelves that were anchored to the walls and had made the area a library. Their baby dolls even had a small area set up like a nursery. On the wall right behind the door, they had used chalkboard paint so the girls could create whatever they wanted, erase it and start all over again.

"I think they're going to love it," Chessie said, coming into the room alongside him. "This is more than I expected! Now I have to finish up the doll blankets for the cribs that dad made. I've already made them each a throw for when they're curled up on the loveseat watching a movie."

Mack looked down at Chessie in amazement. When did this woman find the time to do that kind of thing? As far as he knew, she worked, went to school and took care of Jade. Voicing that question, he wasn't surprised to hear, "I crochet when I go to bed. Usually I read, but right now, with Christmas coming and working all the hours I am, that's the only time I have."

Grabbing her hand, they left the room, being careful to lock the door so the little girls couldn't peek. The door itself would be changed into a half door. It was already in the garage and they would change it out on Christmas Eve once the girls went to bed. And Sam had crafted a wooden piece that would go over the door and along the wall so that it looked like they were walking into a house. There was even a little sign on one side that said "Sophie and Jade's Playhouse" and a small, usable mailbox.

"Pixie-girl, I don't think you guys will get the girls out of that room once they see what's in there!" he said.

Laughing, she said, "Yeah, we figured as much. But we also figured that as they grew up, we could change it and eventually, make it a room where they and their friends could hang out, y'know?"

"Yeah, I can see that happening. So, whose house is it anyhow?" he asked.

"It belongs to the three of us. Mom and dad helped us with the down payment, but it's in our names, not theirs."

"So…what happens when you or Pam or Fran get married?" he queried.

"Well, depending on the man and his circumstances, they would either live here with built-in roommates, or we would move in with them. The house will stay in our names regardless because we want the girls to have something when they get older."

Ah, that makes sense he thought. *And it's not like I cannot duplicate this in my own house because I am going to want my pixie to myself for a while.*

"What has that look on your face Mack?" she asked.

"Oh just thinking, Pixie-girl."

"About?"

"About how if this is going where I think it is, you better be prepared to move."

Move? Shit, they had gone on one date! Holy moly!

Displaying none of this on her face, she simply said, "Wherever my husband is, I will follow."

Drawing her close with his hands around her waist, he leaned down and gently kissed her. "Ah my Pixie-girl, that's the answer I was hoping for if you want the truth."

"Mack, I'll always want to hear the truth, even if it's hard to hear."

"As do I. I think honesty and communication is a good foundation for a relationship. It builds trust. Now that we've done all this work, what say we go pick up that little sprite and go get something to eat? And I heard there was a new kid-oriented movie out. Do you think she'd want to go?"

OMG. This man was killing her!

"Yes, let's go get her and see what she thinks about taking in a show."

As he helped her with her jacket, he was thinking about later. He wanted her, but not just for one night. Now, how to convince her?

Chapter Twelve

"Momma! Today we made snowball cookies!" Jade cried when she saw her mother and Mack walk through the door at Sadie's house.

Looking at her daughter and seeing the streaks of confectioner's sugar covering her cheeks, she reached out a finger and swiped it down her face and licking it, said, "I see that, pumpkin. Are you sure that *you* are not a snowball?"

Mack watched as the little girl broke out in giggles. She took delight in so many things and it was obvious that her mother doted on her.

"Mister Mack wants to take us to dinner and to see that new movie that came out," Chessie told her daughter.

Wide eyes stared up at him. "Really?"

"Yes, really, my little sprite! Are you ready to go or do you need to help your grandma clean up?"

"No we cleaned as we went. Grandma Sadie said that way, when everything is done, you're done too!" Jade said. "I gotta wash my face first, okay?"

"Of course, pumpkin."

Goodbyes said, a missing glove located and face clean, they finally headed out to Mack's truck, where he helped both of his girls in and made sure Jade was buckled up before he headed to the driver's seat. "What are you two in the mood to eat?"

Chapter Thirteen

As Chessie got Jade settled after the busy evening, she thought back over the past few days. She knew, somehow, that Mack was different than anyone she had ever met. He had a very commanding presence, yet his calmness made her feel safe and secure. Listening to Jade talk about the movie and how much fun she had, and seeing the delight that crossed her daughter's face, had her making a decision that would hopefully benefit both of their futures.

"Alright, pumpkin. Time for you to go to sleep, okay? Momma has to work tomorrow so I have to get in bed too, okay?"

"Okay Momma. I love you."

"Ah, my sweet girl, I love you too, so very much. Sleep tight and I'll see you in the morning, okay?"

Going back to her room and getting settled for the night, she had just picked up her crocheting to see if she could get something closer to being finished when she heard a soft knock on her door. "Come in," she said softly.

At her call, the door opened and she saw her two best friends waltz in, already in pajamas and dragging their pillows and two bottles of wine. Not an unusual sight at all as they had often pig-piled in one room or another, drinking wine, gossiping and watching whatever sappy chick flick they could find.

"We figured we haven't done this in a while and we want to know *all* about Mack!" Pam cried, claiming the middle of the bed. Dammit, she was a bed hog. Thank goodness for a California King.

"Yeah, fill us in now that the girls are sleeping and there are no men around to distract any of us," Fran said, after pouring them each a healthy glass of wine.

"Hmm, what do you two want to know?" Chessie asked cautiously, because with these two, the sky was the limit.

"How is he in bed?"

"What's it like after all these years?"

"Do you think he's a keeper?"

Holy shit. They were tripping over themselves asking these questions and already her head was spinning and she hadn't taken the first sip of wine!

"Okay. Let's see. We haven't had sex yet. Yes, he spent the night here, but we talked and that was it. He doesn't want to move too fast. And yes, I do think he's a keeper. What do you two think?"

Fran thought for a minute then said, "Y'know, the way he has had his eye on you these past few days, I can see him being here for the long haul."

"What happened to our 'try before you buy' plan we had?" Pam butted in.

"Yeah, because that worked out so fucking well for me before," Chessie shot back. "I'll definitely have sex with him. He's hot and interested and it's been a long dry spell and he's the first one who has had me even thinking about it at all, so why not?"

Continuing on, she said, "He is good with both of the girls, Mom and Dad obviously like him and know of his family, and he and your guys all got along, right?"

Silent contemplation from them both had her raising her brows. "What?"

"I don't think you were this hot and bothered back when you and Jason were a thing," Fran finally said.

"Hmm, you're right! She wasn't!" Pam chimed in.

"Okay so now that we have my love life on track, what about you two?"

"Ah…well, I think I'm done playing the field," Pam said. "Derek has been interested in me for a long time, but he said he waited until I settled down a bit."

Chessie thought for a moment. Yeah, she could see him waiting for her free-spirited friend to realize that miscellaneous hook-ups were not what she wanted. "Yeah I can see that and I am so happy for you and Sophie both!" she cried.

"What about Aaron? You said you two were back on again?" Chessie queried.

"Uh, yeah. We're both tired of playing games and are talking about moving in together," Fran admitted.

"Wow, really? I'm happy for you. I know it's something you've wanted for a long time now," Chessie said.

"The hard part is going to be leaving you two."

"As if! You'll see us at the diner and I'm sure we'll all go out together. Plus, we're supposed to be going on our weeklong vacation between Christmas and New Year's, remember?"

"About that–do you think the guys could come along?" Fran asked.

"Well…the house we rented *is* big enough. I guess I can talk to Mack to see if he would want to come with us and if he doesn't, I just won't go so I'm not a third wheel for you two and your beaus," Chessie responded.

"Ha! I don't think he will say no, my friend!" Pam cried.

"Oh really?"

"Yeah. Really."

"I guess we will see, won't we? Now, what are we going to watch?"

Chapter Fourteen

Looking around the room, Mack paused. *Would she like it? Was it too soon?* He had recreated the playroom at his house so that Jade would have her own space whenever they were at his house, which he hoped would be soon. Closing his eyes, he could picture the little girl playing and singing and just having a good time. Now that this was done, he could take a quick shower and go see his girl. *His girl. Shit if his buddies could hear his thoughts, they'd take his man card and have a bonfire going before he could deny otherwise. Ah, who cares,* he thought. *It wasn't as if he was eighteen and green around the ears. His military service had allowed him to go places and experience things most only dreamed of. Now? He was ready to settle down.*

Shower done, he walked back through his room to grab some warm clothes. The temperatures had dropped even further, and the snow that had fallen was still there and the newscasters were saying something about unprecedented amounts of snow heading their way. Might not be a bad idea to hit the grocery store and stock up, just in case. As he dressed, he wondered how best to pursue his pixie. He thought about it while preparing a travel mug of coffee, and again as he headed to his truck. Thank goodness for automatic starters, especially in the bone-chilling temperatures.

Making his way through the grocery store, he picked up some kid-friendly items as well for Jade. Then he wondered if their house was stocked up against the pending weather. Well, he could run to the diner-as cold as it was out, nothing was going to spoil.

***

"Order up!" Joe called out.

"I've got it," Chessie told Fran. "You go ahead and top off coffee and I'll bring it on over. Table four, right?"

"Yeah. Thanks girl!"

"No problem." Walking back to table four with a tray, she saw Mack come in the door. The smile that lit up his face took her breath away. "Mack, hey! We're all over today so just grab a seat and I'll be there in a few, okay?" she called out.

"That's fine, Pixie-girl!"

Finished at table four, she hurried over to Mack. "You look cold!"

"Ah, I know a way I could get warm quickly if you're of a mind, that is," he said, smirking.

Blushing, she looked at him and said, "Well, now might not be a good time for that considering where we are!"

He laughed then leaned over and gave her a quick kiss. "I'll take the special, beautiful. What are you doing later?"

"Well, I have more to wrap so was going to do that since mom and dad have the girls for their traditional 'watch Christmas movies' marathon tonight. Want to help?"

"My wrapping leaves much to be desired but I'd love to come and help you by handing you tape and paper," he responded.

"That works too! I'll get this order in for you. Do you want some coffee?"

"Please. And, Chessie? The weather is getting bad, you be careful coming home later, okay?"

"I will. I promise."

***

Later that day

As Chessie walked out to her car, she could see that the snow had been falling steadily, and from the looks of things, it wasn't going to let up any time soon. At this rate, they were going to be snowed in for Christmas! Shaking her head, she cranked the car then waited as it warmed up. With the weather the way it was, traffic was light, but she was still careful going through town as the plows hadn't been able to keep up with the snowfall. As her ten-minute drive stretched to fifteen and then twenty minutes, she wondered if she had missed her turn, then shook her head. How silly! Of course she didn't, she was simply driving slower than normal. Ah, finally, there was their driveway. She hummed in pleasure when she saw that Mack's truck was already there. She was hoping she could talk him into spending the night since the girls weren't there. The weather would be the perfect excuse!

Gathering the bags from her trunk, she made her way into the house and saw Mack walking towards her, his hands out to take what she had. Once he had put them on the couch in the family room, he came back and helped her get out of her coat. Giving her a quick kiss on her forehead, he said, "Go. Get comfortable. I put a pot of beef vegetable soup on when I got over here and I want to feed my girl before she starts wrapping!"

Laughing, she winked at him and said. "I may need my strength for more than wrapping!"

***

Heading back into the kitchen after changing clothes, she took a second to appreciate the fact that a man was standing in *her* kitchen, dishing out food that he had made. For her. "Mmm, it smells so darned good! I can't wait to eat," she said, coming up behind him and wrapping her arms around his waist.

He froze. This was the first time she had willingly put her hands on him and he wasn't going to blow it. Putting the bowls that he had filled down, he turned in her arms carefully, hugging her back as he leaned in and gave her a quick kiss. "Where are your socks?" he said, peering down at the bare feet sticking out from beneath a pair of fuzzy lounge pants.

"Oops. Well, if I'm honest, I don't like anything on my feet," she said.

"Don't your toes get cold?"

"Yeah, sometimes."

"Well, eat first, then you can get some, okay? Last thing you want to do is get sick right before Jade's birthday and Christmas!"

Good heavens, a man who made sense. Sitting down, she waited for him to grab their bowls, and then she took her first bite. "Oh my goodness, Mack! This is delicious!"

He grinned at her as she continued to spoon the soup into her mouth. "Glad you like it, Pixie-girl. My mother made sure all of her children could cook."

"I like to cook as well, but enjoy baking more," she said, while buttering a piece of the bread he had made. Heaven. She had died and gone to culinary heaven.

Hearing the low moan that she made as she chewed had him wondering if she would make that same noise in bed. He was so lost in his thoughts about her in bed that he didn't hear her until she called his name again.

"Mack? You okay?"

"What? Yes, just thinking about something. Sorry about that, Pixie-girl."

"What were you thinking? The look on your face was rather…intriguing."

Throwing caution to the wind, he looked at her and said, "How you'll sound when we're in bed together, Pixie-girl."

Cue the blush she thought. "Oh. I…see," she stammered.

"Chessie, it'll happen at some point and while I'm man enough to admit I wish it was now, I'm also man enough to tell you that it's when you're ready, yeah?" he softly said.

"What if…if I'm ready now? I mean, I know we've only known each other for a matter of days, but I've never felt what I'm feeling before for anyone else and I want to see where it goes."

"Let's roll with it, okay, Pixie-girl? No pressure. I know you've got some wrapping to do, and the weather is shit so I wasn't planning to go anywhere tonight anyhow."

"Okay, no pressure," she finally said after looking at him closely to see that indeed, he meant what he said. If they did, they did. If they waited, he was okay with that as well.

With dinner finally finished and the kitchen cleaned up, he shooed her to get a pair of socks for her feet while he set up a table in her family room to make it easier for her to wrap.

"What? Oh! That will be a lot easier, Mack! Usually, my back is about half dead before I'm all done, bending over on the floor."

Coming close to her, he drew her into his arms and before his mouth found hers, he said, "I'm all about making your life easier, Pixie-girl."

Holy smokes could he kiss!

Chapter Fifteen

Mack built up the fire so they would stay warm and found a channel playing Christmas movies while she got out a few bags, the wrapping paper, tape and bows. Getting comfortable on the couch, she separated the gifts according to who they were for and then started wrapping.

As she wrapped, they talked about the renovations he was making and had already made to his house. She couldn't wait to see what he had done.

"Pixie-girl? I uh…I went ahead and converted one of the rooms into a playroom for Jade at my house," he finally told her.

"Really? She's going to be so excited!"

"I thought you might be upset."

"Why would I be upset?" she asked him quizzically.

"Well…I got to thinking that you might think it was presumptuous of me to do something like that since we just met a few days ago. But honestly? I feel like I've known you forever," he told her.

Putting the tape down, she crawled across the couch to where he was sitting and didn't stop until she was straddling his lap. Wrapping her arms around his neck, she told him between kisses, "Mack Corrigan, I think Santa sent you to me a few weeks early."

Pulling her flush against his chest, he gently cupped her face in one of his hands and while stroking her cheek, he softly replied, "I think you're right, my sweet pixie-girl," before he lowered his head and claimed her lips in a blistering kiss.

As the movie played on and the fire continued to burn, he made love to her mouth, while his hands roamed across her back. With their kisses growing more fervent, he realized that he wasn't prepared to take it further and he stopped for a second, saying, "Pixie-girl, not prepared to take this further tonight even though I want to."

She could feel how much he wanted to and knew that she was in the same boat desire-wise. Blowing out a breath, she softly said, "And I'm not on anything, either, dammit!"

He chuckled at her frustration and said, "We'll figure it out. Now, what has to be hidden and what can go under the tree?" She untangled herself from his lap and started pointing at the piles and smiled as he began moving things where they needed to go.

**

Watching her, he fell a little more. He could tell how much she loved the season and he marveled at how well-adjusted she was despite all she had gone through. "Pixie-girl, you want something to drink?"

"That would be great but I'll get it for us because I need to stretch." As she went into the kitchen, she glanced out the window and called out, "Mack, you should see how much snow has fallen!"

He came behind her and pulled her into him, wrapping his arms around her waist. "Pixie-girl, looks like a winter wonderland out there, I'm glad I won't be going anywhere tonight."

She smiled inside–she had loved waking up in his arms and wouldn't complain about the weather keeping him with her. Breaking away after giving him a quick kiss, she grabbed the phone and sent a quick text to Pam.

Chessie: Hey girl, you're staying put, yeah?

Pam: Yep.

Chessie: Question for you.

Pam: What?

Chessie: Well, Mack is here…

Pam: And?

Chessie: Um, do you have any condoms?

Pam: OMG!!! Hell yeah, in my night stand. The drought is O-V-E-R!

Chessie: Hahaha. Very funny. I just want to be prepared is all.

Pam: Have fun chica!

***

When the lights flickered for the fourth time, Mack went and got more wood while Chessie made sure the bathrooms had water in the tubs and hunted down flashlights. They were on city water, but always made sure to fill up the tubs to flush the toilets. Meeting back in the family room with some blankets and pillows, she looked at him and said, "Figured we might have to bunk out here."

"Good idea, Pixie-girl."

He went and got the air mattress from the spare room and together they got the bed made.

"Uh, Mack?"

He looked at her in the firelight and his first thought was *mine* followed by curiosity at the tone she was using. Standing, he pulled her into his arms–something he was becoming addicted to–and leaning his forehead against hers said, "What is it, Pixie-girl?"

He watched as her face flushed and she took a deep breath. "I uh…I texted Pam a little while ago."
"And?" he asked her, wondering why.

"She...uh...she has some condoms, so uh...well..." she stammered out, unable to meet his eyes.

Understanding dawned on him and he leaned down to whisper, "Did she tell you where they are?"

"Mmhmm," she responded.

"Well, my vote is you go grab them so we have them handy," he said as he nipped her earlobe.

"Okay. Uh, I'm gonna grab a shower before we lose power totally and I'll get them then."

"Sounds like a plan, my Pixie-girl."

***

She was almost done with her shower when the lights flickered again before going out completely. *Shit* she thought as she turned off the water and carefully got out of the stall. She might have forgotten a flashlight but her towel and clothes were laid out at least. As she quickly dried off, she could hear Mack come into the room.

"Pixie-girl? Brought you a flashlight. You doing okay?"

Slipping into her flannel pajama set, she said, "Yeah, almost done, you can come in."

He opened the bathroom door and burst into laughter at the sight in front of him.

"What's so funny?"

"Pixie-girl, I hope I'm not sounding too forward when I say this, but I love the reindeer."

She looked down and realized that the noses on the two reindeer were over her nipples. Raising her eyebrows, she said, "You do?"

With a husky tone in his voice, he came closer and leaned down to whisper, "Oh yeah, my Pixie-girl, I honestly do."

Gah his voice she thought. It was turning her insides to goo. "C'mon, let's get back to the family room so you stay warm," he told her.

She finished running a brush through her hair as he reached out his hand for her. Once back in the family room after detouring into Pam's room, he got her settled then told her he was going to close the other doors to conserve the house's heat. Looking up at him, she thanked him and then sent off quick texts to the girls and her parents to make sure all were accounted for and safe and sound.

He made quick work of a shower in the dark and then closed the other doors and made sure the house was locked down before he rejoined her. Laying side by side on the air mattress, he traced her face with his thumb and index finger before he leaned down to capture her lips in a quick kiss. "Pixie-girl, nowhere else I'd rather be than right here with you right now," he told her as his thumb and index finger continued to caress her cheek and jawline.

Looking at him, she softly replied, "Same here, Mack. I don't understand the connection we have but I'm not going to question it."

In the glow of the firelight, he could see how her eyes were shining. Leaning in, he softly kissed her–first her forehead and then each cheek before he captured her lips. Passion soon flared and he pulled her closer, cupping the back of her neck with one hand while the other stroked along her back and down her side.

Time stood still while they caressed and kissed. He could feel her restless movements against him and broke their kiss to say, "Pixie-girl, I want to see you."

She pulled back slightly and then shyly lifted her pajama top, stopping when he took over. He looked at her–full breasts with pebbled nipples- and he leaned down and nuzzled first one and then the other. Her soft moans filled the air even as she looked at him with wonder in her eyes. "Mack," she breathed out on a sigh.

"I've got you, Pixie, and I won't let go," he promised as his thumb stroked the nipple before he brought his mouth down to capture it between his lips.

Oh my God she thought as shocks of pleasure went through her. Reaching out blindly, she fisted his T-shirt struggling to get to his skin. He pulled back slightly and in a move that only men seemed capable of pulled the shirt off over his head and tossed it to the side. *Oh heavens* she thought as she felt the warmth of his skin against her chest. She lifted one hand and traced his chest from shoulder to waist, feeling the slight tickle of his chest hairs and she marveled at how it felt beneath her fingers. He was so warm, radiating a heat that was causing the inferno within to flame even higher.

"Mack…Mack?" she stammered out.

"Hmm, Pixie?" he whispered, dropping a kiss below her ear that had her shivering.

"I…I want more," she admitted. "But…"

"But what, Pixie-girl?" he asked gently, laying back and pulling her so she was partially across his chest.

"I…" she faltered and then he watched as she took in a breath and carried on, "I don't really know what to do. I mean, I don't want to bring him into this, but it was only the one time and I sure as hell didn't feel like I'm feeling right now."

Smiling down at her as he could feel how her body was reacting, he kissed her on the nose and said, "Do whatever feels right, Pixie. Do whatever you want. We'll figure out as we go what you like, and I'll tell you and show you what I enjoy, okay?"

She thought about what he had just said and finally nodded her head. "I want to touch you."

He laid back against the pillows and said, "Have at it, my sweet Pixie."

Leaning up, she looked down at the man lying there. She could see how dark his eyes were and a thrill of something she couldn't name ran through her. *She* was the reason he was looking like he was, no one else! Reaching out a hand, she traced his face with her fingers before she began stroking his arms and chest. *Ah that chest* she thought. Muscles that weren't overboard but were testament to how he cared for himself. Chest hair that wasn't too much and wasn't too little–she giggled thinking "just right" as she lowered to tease one of his nipples peeking through with her tongue. A hiss of indrawn breath had her glancing up only to hear him say, "Feels good, Pixie." Emboldened now, she continued her perusal, occasionally touching and stroking and kissing. She could see the evidence of his desire against the sweats he wore and wondered how it was going to feel. Running a finger underneath the waistband, she felt his indrawn breath, but he didn't say anything so she continued. As she attempted to pull them down, he finally came to life beneath her and within seconds, he was lying there naked. Now sitting back on her knees, she looked at all he had to offer and was thrilled at the fact that he wanted her. Reaching out her hand, she gently grasped his erection and gasped at the contrast of silky smooth skin covering hot molten steel. Stroking gently, she felt his hand cover hers and heard him say, "Like this, Pixie" as he tightened her hold on him. The soft skin below his bellybutton beckoned her and she leaned down to nuzzle the skin and lave it with her tongue, continuing the motion he had shown her.

I'm in heaven he thought as he watched her through hooded eyes. He wanted to take over but instinctively knew that she needed to do this and he silently cursed Jason for his ineptitude even as he thanked the heavens that *he* was going to be teaching her about all things pleasurable. Shifting slightly to his side, he brought her back down careful not to break her connection with his straining cock and he captured her lips in a passion-filled kiss.

Heaven she thought as he continued to kiss her while his hands moved to remove the rest of her pajamas. When they were both lying there naked, he looked at her and seeing the worry in her eyes, he said, "Pixie, you're beautiful. You'll be beautiful when we are old and gray and gravity has taken over."

He traced the silvery stretch marks that she had on her hips, marveling again at the strength she had, and then leaned down and traced them with his tongue. Hearing her indrawn breath, he smiled against her skin as he said, "Pixie-girl, you are intoxicating me. Let me get a taste."

Holy hell in a handbasket she thought as he maneuvered so he was between her thighs. Jason had never…and then she stopped thinking and started feeling. His hands, his lips, his tongue-all were stroking her *there* and she felt like she was soaring through the sky. "Mack," she moaned.

He continued his gentle assault on her knowing it had been a long time and that she had likely never had any pleasure. Feeling her body react to what he was doing, hearing her soft moans and mewls, he knew it wasn't going to be long before she shattered.

Minutes. Hours. Days. She lost track of time as he brought her body to a fevered pitch. Feeling as if she were going to fall over a cliff, she cried out and heard him say, "Come for me, Pixie-girl," before she shattered in a million pieces.

***

He let her ride out her orgasm and when he felt the tremors start to subside, he made his way back up her body, nipping, kissing and stroking, until he captured her lips in his once again. He could taste the salt from tears she didn't know were falling, and he made quick work rolling on the condom. "You ready, Pixie-girl?" he asked as he ran his cock through the wetness at her thighs.

"Mmhmm," she answered, looking at him through hooded eyes.

As he slowly entered and filled her, he kept her eyes. He saw the slight flare as he slowly entered her and leaned his forehead against hers. "You okay, Pixie?" he panted out.

"Better than okay, Mack. Feels so good," she replied.

Fully seated, he moaned. "So warm and tight, my Pixie-girl. Feels like I've come home."

She marveled at how he filled and stretched her. Not like she was an expert, but he seemed above average and the feeling of fullness permeated her down to the bones. Moving slightly, she moaned when he captured one of her legs and put it around his hips before he began to pull back.

With both legs now wrapped around his hips and waist, she moaned as he began moving, setting a steady pace that was intoxicating. He leaned down and began kissing her, mimicking with his lips and tongue what he was doing to her with his cock.

As the fire continued to burn, they continued the dance older than time. Sweat began to glisten on their bodies and he increased his rhythm. Moans and pants filled the air and she could feel herself climbing once again toward that cliff. "Mack!" she cried out as her orgasm overtook her. As she was riding it out, she felt him stiffen above her before he called out her name as he captured her lips once again.

***

He had gotten up and taken care of the condom and found a cloth that he warmed before he cleaned her up. Now laying in his arms, sated and a bit sleepy, she ran her fingers idly across his chest before saying, "Wow. I've got no other words besides that."

He chuckled lightly before placing a kiss on her forehead. "That sums it up for me as well, Pixie."

"I didn't…I mean…I never realized it could be that good," she finally said.

"It's never been that good for me either," he told her. "Not gonna lie and say I've been a monk, because I haven't, but it's pretty much always been a means to an end. I've never felt for anyone what I'm feeling for you, my Pixie-girl, and if I feel like this in just a few short days, I'm looking forward to seeing what the future holds."

"Well, you know my history, so you know it's never been like that for me," she said.

"I know and I gotta be honest when I say I'm looking forward to showing you more."

More? Holy shit. She had hit the mother-freaking lottery she thought in wonder. "I think I'm going to enjoy that quite a bit."

He chuckled then said, "Pixie-girl, as much as I want to lay here with you naked in my arms, since we have no power, think we both need to get dressed again, then I'm going to put some more wood on the fire."

Chapter Sixteen
Christmas Eve

What a week she thought. They had been snowed in for three days, pretty much shutting the town down. Mack had taken her in to town so she could help at the diner with the people who had been stuck with no way home. He had even helped in the kitchen while she took care of the customers. And the nights? She blushed thinking of all the ways he had made love to her already. He was everything she never knew she needed-kind, compassionate, passionate, loving-she felt desired, cherished and dare she even think it? Loved. And he adored Jade, showering the little girl with affection. She sighed with happiness as she worked to finish Jade's birthday cake. Everyone would be there in a few hours for dinner and cake before they headed off to midnight mass. And because of the "big reveal of the playroom", they were going to have a house full of people-Mom and Dad, Derek, Aaron, and Mack were all staying the night. *Blessed*. That one word kept running through her mind.

Hearing a noise, she turned and saw Pam coming through the door, cheeks rosy from the cold wintery day. "Hey you! Are you ready with our earplugs for tomorrow morning?" her friend asked as she brought in drinks and stuff for Christmas morning breakfast. Dad had insisted on providing dinner so that they could enjoy the party and she wasn't going to argue.

"Ha! Smartass. Guess your new man has brought that out to the forefront, yeah?"

"Whatevs. Hey, what do you think of the cake?"

Pam looked at it and marveled at the hidden talents of her friend. "Girl, it almost looks too good to eat!"
"I hope she likes it."

"I think she'll love it!"

"Okay, I have a few more things to get wrapped and then I have to get ready. You good here?"

"Yeah, I've got this, you go do what you have to do."

Giving Pam a quick hug, she hurried off to her room. With Mack around, it had been challenging to finish his gift and it had finally dried so she could get it wrapped. *I can't wait to cuddle with him under this* she thought as she looked over the cable stitched afghan. Gathering her wrapping tools, she set about getting the afghan wrapped along with a few other items, then got them under the tree. Looking around the family room, her face flushed thinking of the week prior. She turned the tree lights on and sighed at how pretty it looked-they let the girls help every year and Mom had started a tradition when Jade and Sophie were born of giving them each a unique ornament for the Christmas tree. Seeing the years of love displayed so prominently on the tree had her smiling at the memories each evoked. Again the word blessed rolled through her soul.

Warm arms wrapped around her and a husky voice rasped in her ear, "Hey my Pixie-girl. I think this is my favorite room after last week."

Turning, she looked up into the eyes of the man who had captured her heart. Who cared if it was "too soon"? She leaned up and gave him a kiss before saying, "Mine too, Mack."

"So what do you need help with?"

"Well, I've got the cake done and the dining room decorated, the last minute gifts have been wrapped, and Sam sent dinner with Pam, so the only thing I have left is to take a shower and get ready," she replied.

"I think I can help you with that, Pixie-girl," he said as he led her to her room.

***

Two hours later, sated and relaxed, they waited for everyone to show up. Hearing car doors slamming had her getting up and going to the door, only to burst out laughing. Seemed that the birthday girl had gotten a bouquet of balloons and they were attempting to defeat her as she carried them into the house.

"Momma! Look what Grandpa got me!"

"They're beautiful, sweetie. Here let me take them and I'll have Mack tie them up someplace safe, okay?"

"Okay, Momma."

As the adults came in with steaming pans filled with pasta, garlic bread, and salad, she started getting the plates put together. Soon, everyone was sitting down and enjoying baked ziti, one of Jade's favorite foods. "Momma, when are we doing cake?"

"Once we're done with dinner and have it cleaned up, we will do your presents and then cake, how's that?"

"That might be a good idea, Momma, because I'm kind of full."

Laughter broke out around the table at the earnest look on the little girl's face. "Mr. Mack, before I open up my presents, can you give Momma her 'prise?"

Chessie looked over at Mack and saw the slight blush cover his cheeks. "Yeah, Sprite, we can do that if you're sure?"

"Oh yes, it was one of my birthday *and* Christmas wishes!"

Chessie raised her eyebrows at Mack and mouthed, "What did you do?"

He just smiled and wouldn't answer.

***

Dinner finished, they all gathered in the family room, Jade going over to sit by Mack. As the room quietened, Chessie found him on one knee in front of her and her heart stopped. "Mack? What…what are you doing?"

Opening up the small velvet box he had pulled from his pocket, he said, "With this ring, I'm promising you some things, Pixie-girl. I promise that, when the time is right, I will be asking you to marry me. I promise that I will love, cherish and adore you until my last breath. I promise that I will love Jade as my own, and work to give her brothers and sisters. I promise that I will always take care of you. I promise that you'll be the first person I see in the morning and the last thing I think about after kissing you goodnight. I promise to never change the essence of you. I promise to bring you chocolate, flowers and wine on those days of the month when you need them most. And I promise you that the desire burning in me will only grow stronger. Will you wear my ring?"

By now, Chessie had tears rolling silently down her face. This man had come into her life two short weeks ago and turned her world upside down. She knew, to her bones, that he was a good, solid man and that everything he had just said was already engraved on his heart. For her. *For her!* Reaching out and sliding her hand along his jaw, she softly said, "Yes. I don't care if people think it's too soon. I felt the attraction to you that very first day and believe that you'll keep every one of those promises. Now, I have a few promises of my own for you, Mack. I promise you that I'll always be by your side as your partner, lover and helpmate. I promise to love you until my last breath. I promise to help you fill our home with laughter and love and children. I promise to never take what we have for granted, but to nurture it so it continues to grow."

Hearing her words, Mack crushed her to him and, reaching up he threaded one hand into her hair while the other stroked her cheek before he claimed her lips. Love, passion, desire – it was all evident in how he worshipped her lips with his own.

Epilogue – Two Years Later
New Year's Eve

As she waited for her husband to get home, a secret smile played on her lips. Today was their first anniversary and they were celebrating it privately before they went to a party down at the diner. She looked around at her home-their home-and marveled at the renovations he had made. The house was a home in every sense of the word and filled with love and laughter and hope. Going into the family room and sitting back down, she was gazing at the Christmas tree when she felt his presence right before he slipped his arms around her shoulder and leaned in to whisper, "Hey, Pixie-girl."

She turned in his arms so she could kiss him hello. As was typical with them, a quick kiss quickly heated up and she found herself breathless and anxious to start the anniversary festivities. "Handsome, you keep that up and we'll be under the Christmas tree."

"And that's a problem how?"

Laughing, she looked at him and replied, "Actually, it's not since we're here alone. Jade went with Mom down to the diner to "decorate" so we've got a few hours for just us, if you're interested."

If he was interested he thought. There wasn't a time in the day that he wasn't interested in loving on his wife. Reaching for her hand, he drew them over to the Christmas tree and started laughing when he saw that the air mattress was already there waiting for them. Laying down with his wife, he faced her and placed a soft kiss on her nose.

"Uh, Mack? I've got another Christmas gift for you. I know it's a week late but…"

Curious, he raised up and looked closely at her and could see her eyes sparkling. "What is it, Pixie-girl?"

She reached into her pocket and drew out a long thin box and handed it to him. Holding her breath, she watched him open it and stare at the contents. When he finally looked at her, there was wonder on his face as he said, "Pixie-girl? We're going to have a baby?"

"Yes, handsome, we are. Merry Christmas and Happy Anniversary."

Cupping her face in his hands, he kissed her gently before whispering, "Happy Anniversary, Pixie-girl. I love you now and forever."

***Merry Christmas!
May your holiday
season be blessed
beyond measure!***

About the Author

Darlene is a transplanted Yankee, moving from upstate New York when she was a teenager. She lives with the brat-cat pack and a small muffin dog, all rescues, as she plots and plans who will get to "talk" next!

Find me on Facebook!

https://www.facebook.com/darlenetallmanauthor/

Want to read my first book, "Bountiful Harvest"? You can get it here:

http://myBook.to/BountifulHarvest

And my second book, "His Firefly", which just released 11/3/16:

http://myBook.to/HisFirefly

Made in the USA
Columbia, SC
15 January 2024